Industrial Narrow Gauge
Stock and Trackwork

Sydney A. Leleux

Plateway Press

ISBN 1 871980 53 4

ISBN 1 871980 53 4

PLATEWAY PRESS
Taverner House, Harling Road, East Harling, Norfolk NR16 2QR

Printed in England by POSTPRINT
Taverner House, Harling Road, East Harling, Norfolk NR16 2QR

FRONT COVER / TITLE PAGE ILLUSTRATION

Bedford Silica Sand Mines, Heath & Reach near Leighton Buzzard, had a 2ft gauge line in its sand
pit. Here a train of Hudson skips is being emptied into a waiting lorry from a typical tipping dock.
Motor Rail locomotives were common in quarries, although cabs were usually fitted. This is number
8592 (29-6-1961).

BACK COVER ILLUSTRATION

Kettering Furnaces was still digging some iron ore manually until the 1950s, and even when a face
shovel was brought into the last remaining quarry there was still hard manual work to be done.
Trains ran in pairs, two pairs in the morning and one in the afternoon. The locomotive of the first
train left its 24 empty wagons in a loop at the quarry and collected half of the full wagons. It then
waited in a second quarry loop for the other train to arrive and then left for the works. The second
locomotive hauled the remaining loaded wagons from the quarry into a loop and then pushed all
the empties into the quarry past the excavator. It then left with the second loaded train for the
works. Empties were pushed up to the excavator, loaded, and then pushed out of the way (8-1-
1962). As starting a wagon loaded with 2 tons of ore could be very hard work, the excavator driver
sometimes positioned his bucket behind the wagon body and slewed his machine, thus nudging the
wagon into motion. It was easier for the men but caused a lot of damage to wagon body planks.
When several wagons had been filled, the face shovel was slewed towards the empties and the
shovel arm racked out. A wire rope was hooked to the bucket and to the leading wagon, and the
driver slewed the excavator, pulling the empties nearer so the men did not have so far to push them
into position for loading.

Contents

Introduction

Reports of visits to industrial railways frequently describe the current locomotive position in detail but often pay scant regard to the rolling stock they haul. If there is any mention, it is likely to be on the lines of 'Two rakes each of 6 V-skips, one in use and the other spare'. This is a pity, as the rolling stock can be as interesting as the locomotives – or even more interesting in some cases! While I have visited a number of industrial narrow gauge railways without locomotives, I have never yet been to an operating system which had no rolling stock.

Narrow gauge railways – that is having a gauge of less than the standard one of 4ft 8 $^1/_2$in – cover a very wide range. The first edition of the Industrial Railway Society (IRS) Pocket Book EL (Existing Locomotives) published in January 1969 listed British locomotive-operated industrial railways using no less than 35 different gauges, ranging from 1ft 3in to 4ft 6in. Surface railways in collieries alone used no less than 17 different gauges, from 1ft 9in to 3ft 6in. While 2ft or thereabouts was by far the commonest gauge, it was by no means the only one.

This little book does not pretend to be a definitive account of British narrow gauge industrial rolling stock, but merely to give an indication of the enormous variety of equipment that used to be found. Regrettably, most of the lines illustrated have now passed into history, and this may be their only record and memorial. However, if it shows that the train behind the locomotive is often worthy of attention in its own right (and this is true no matter what the gauge, and whether the railway is industrial, public passenger carrying or miniature), then it will have served a useful purpose. Incidentally, the track is often worth a second glance too, and it generally receives even less attention than the rolling stock, although it is a fundamental part of any railway!

If you enjoy this book, and want to learn more about narrow gauge railways, you could join the Narrow Gauge Railway Society (founded 1951), Secretary: Brian Gent, 34 East Street, Fareham, Hampshire PO16 0BY.

Unless otherwise stated, all the photographs were taken by the author.

My thanks go to my publisher, Andrew Neale, who was so responsive when I suggested the book to him and who has encouraged me during its preparation. As always, I must thank my wife Zoe. This time I think I have surprised her by producing the book in *less* time than I forecast!

Sydney A. Leleux
Stanton-by-Dale
Ilkeston
Derbyshire

April 2004

Skips

Many industrial narrow gauge railways carried loose material in bulk, so ease of unloading was important. One of the commonest types of wagon, certainly in recent years, was the V-skip, named after the cross section of its tipping body. While Robert Hudson of Leeds was by far the largest British manufacturer it did not have a monopoly. For example, Allen of Tipton, Staffordshire, was quite a common manufacturer. Furthermore, in addition to variations due to manufacturer and gauge, the size and shape of the body, the body catch mechanism, and the design of the frames were some of the reasons behind the variety of designs which were to be found. One could nearly fill a book just with skips!

1. 2ft gauge skips by Allen at Smith & Son (Raunds) Ltd brickworks near Wellingborough (22-7-1964). Note the outward facing flanges on the frame, the curved channel body supports down which the body rolled when it tipped, and the body securing lever hinged at one end of the body support (see the further end of the second skip). Skips left empty for an extended time, for example at the weekend or in a spare rake, often had the body left tipped to prevent it filling with water. The old standard gauge van body behind has had doors cut in the end and is the shed for a small Lister diesel locomotive.

2. Two types of Hudson 2ft gauge skip at Joseph Arnold's Double Arches sand quarry, Leighton Buzzard (14-8-1968). On the nearer wagon, note the channel facing outwards on the frames, the elaborate steel pressing for the body support, and the hinged hoop forming the body catch. The newer type of wagons behind have frames with the channel facing inwards and a simpler design of pressed steel body support.

3. A standard Hudson 2ft gauge skip with the frame extended at one end to give space for a simple brake pillar at George Garside Ltd, Leighton Buzzard (8-1-1960). Such wagons were particularly useful to control trains on down gradients when horse haulage was used.

4. Two different 2ft gauge skips at Earls Barton Silica near Northampton (16-7-1964). The left hand wagon is an Eezitip design by Allen (compare with photograph 1 and spot subtle differences). The right hand skip is by Hudson. It is a standard 1yd^3 skip, but fitted with a trunnion at each end of the body so that it can be lifted off the frame by a crane with a suitable sling and emptied. The U-shaped bar hinged to the top of the body at one end passes either side of the sling, and is hinged back to tip the body. Note the pressed steel legs under the body so that it can be lifted off the frame, put down elsewhere and yet remain upright.

5. Most skips on the smaller gauges used blocks of rubber for springing, but for some reason the 60cm gauge skips owned by the Ministry of Defence at Lydd Ranges, Kent were fitted with coil springs (14-8-1978). Note, too, the lengths of steel tubing used as couplings, to keep wagons apart when being pushed round sharp curves. Beside the skips are some wagons used to carry targets.

6. Redland Felttons Ltd, at Kempston Hardwick brickworks, near Bedford had an extensive 2ft gauge railway. Part of it used 2yd^3 Hudson Rugga design skips, having bodies 70 x 63 max wide x 36in. The central body catches are clearly visible.

7. A fairly typical 2ft gauge 1yd^3 skip, although by a rare manufacturer (McLachlan & Co, Darlington), seen at the fireclay dump belong to Brookes Ltd, Lightcliffe near Halifax (20-9-1967). Some skip manufacturers made the sides slightly lower than the ends to aid loading, particularly by hand. The angle along the body helps to provide strength and protection against impact on the frame when the body tips. The longitudinal strut along the underframe was often provided to help take the stresses caused by locomotive haulage. It was not necessary here, as the skips were pushed by hand.

In December 1950 HUDSON light railway plant was still standard equipment in many small quarries, hence this advertisement in the "Quarry Manager's Journal".

(Andrew Neale collection)

8. Spare rolling stock, and even locomotives, were not always stored in sidings. In this photograph, taken at Rodmell Cement Works, near Lewes, two most unusual skips, plus a body and an underframe without its wheels, lie beside the line where a Ruston diesel (177604) is taking a rake of skips to the quarry. The skips in the foreground have bodies $50^{1}/_{2}$ x 43 x 32in max depth, with 15in radius bottom. The frames were 72 x 34in, with 22in wheelbase and (probably) 12in diameter wheels (19-8-1968).

9. End tipping skips are not common, but several sewage works in Stoke-on-Trent had examples, the one illustrated being at Burslem works (14-6-1971). Basically end tipping skips were made by mounting an ordinary side tipping skip (without wheels) on to an additional wheeled frame at right angles. However, their use was not without problems. Not only did the wagons have to be uncoupled for emptying, and they were wider than normal so clearances at passing loops had to be greater, but also when emptied the load fell over the end of the lower frame and had to be shovelled away. If, as in the example, the wheeled frame was shortened as much as possible (at one or both ends) to prevent the main frames from being burried by the tipped load then it was difficult to couple the wagon to anything else, or push it in a train, as the bodies touched long before the frames did.

(opposite) Adolph Gloster was Orenstein & Koppel's UK agent in the 1930's. After internment during the war he founded Railway Mine & Plantation Ltd to act as export agents for a wide range of light railway and mining plant. This advertisement of February 1949 features a standard "Eezitip" V-skip from W. G. Allen Ltd of Tipton, Staffs. of which RMP handled many thousands over the years.

(Andrew Neale collection)

10. Most skips, except those used on mining systems, had the frames outside the wheels. However, occasionally inside frames would be fitted, such as these 2ft gauge Allen skips at Beswicks Limeworks near Buxton (5-4-1969). Their bodies measured $58^1/_2$ x 50 x 25in. Hudson supplied some very similar wagons here, and yet larger ones but still with inside frames to Leeds sewage works at Knostrop.

11. Mixconcrete Aggregates used a modern 2ft gauge railway at their gravel pits at Charlecote near Stratford on Avon. A 40hp Motor Rail diesel (40S370), then only two years old, hauls a rake of 2yd³ skips in the quarry (7-10-1972). Note the lifting lugs for a crane on the third skip.

12. A standard Husdon skip for 2ft 6in gauge at Eaglescliffe Brickworks, Co.Durham (4-3-1967). Note the use of outward facing steel angle to give the extra width to the frame yet still using the standard ends. The body measured 62 x 63 wide over lip x 30in, with 15in wheels on 36in wheelbase. The overall length was 7ft 6in. The central body catch is clearly visible.

13. Cape Universal Building at Uxbridge had a 2ft 6in gauge line serving their gravel pit (22-8-1968). Here is a rake of high capacity skips, with coil spring suspension, and the end wagon is fitted with a lever operated hand brake acting on all the wheels.

Tippers

Tipping wagons, of which skips in the previous section are a specialised example, used to exist in great variety. Usually for simplicity the wagons tipped to one side only.

14. The Midlands ironstone field used to be the home of a large number of narrow gauge quarry railways. Unlike the slate quarries in North Wales which were remarkably consistent in both gauge and rolling stock, the ironstone lines ranged in gauge from 2ft to 4ft and had very different types of rolling stock. Of the last six quarry lines which survived into the late 1950s, three were 3ft gauge and three metre gauge. Two used wooden side tippers, three used steel tubs and one had high capacity tipplers. The oldest survivor was the 3ft gauge system which served Kettering Furnaces, first put into blast in 1878. The railway continued in operation for a few years after the furnaces were closed until the quarries were worked out. It used wooden side tippers, having a shallow almost square low body (66 x 72 wide x 24in) mounted on a wooden underframe running on $17^{1}/_{2}$ in wheels with $39^{1}/_{2}$ in wheelbase. The single plank door rested on extensions of the body frame to give it support when the body tipped and about 2 tons of ore slid out over it (24-3-1959). Wooden wagons like this were often build by a carpenter based on site.

15. (Opposite Top) Eight miles to the south east, and six miles north of Northampton, was another 3ft gauge line serving the Staveley Iron & Chemical Co's quarries at Scaldwell which dated from 1914. Here were much larger wooden side tippers, with bodies measuring 103 x 72 x $32^{1}/_{2}$ in, with 20in diameter wheels and a wheelbase of 58in. The photograph shows wagons at the tipping dock where standard gauge wagons were loaded. Note the pivoted steel clamps to prevent the wagon overturning when the body tipped, and the sprags on the ground. These lengths of wood, pointed at the ends, were thrust through the spokes of a wheel to act as a brake, and were common on narrow gauge lines (7-9-1961).

16. Dorking Greystone Lime Company at Betchworth near Dorking used a 3ft $2^1/_4$ in gauge railway between the quarry and lime kilns. They used both side and end tipping wagons, and an example of each was preserved at the former Brockham Museum situated in an old quarry close to Betchworth where they were photographed (21-8-1978). Note their very short wheelbase, which was a common feature on old designs of wagon. Note too the considerable overhang at the opening end of the end tipper, which was little hindrance when coupling to a similar vehicle but which made it necessary to use a flat runner if the locomotive had to couple at this end.

17. Alpha Cement at Cliffe near Gravesend had a 2ft gauge line in the chalk quarry which had a wooden body (105 x 68 x 27in) on a sprung steel frame (104^1/$_2$ x 37 x 8 & 12in deep), with 14in diameter wheels at 48in centres. This was photographed at Brockham Museum (21-8-1978).

18. The Marston Valley Brick Co at Ridgmont near Leighton Buzzard had a 2ft 6in gauge railway to bring clay to the works. Originally locomotive worked, it was converted to continuous cable haulage (probably in the late 1940s) with steel side tipping wagons. Note the large buffer on the body but no couplings. Some 1200 wagons per day were manually tipped in this shed. The cable gripper is underneath the wagon (S.V.F.Leleux, 7-6-1968). On straight track rollers were placed at intervals to support the cable – one is just visible immediately beyond the nearer wagon and another is in front of the further wagon. On bends inclined pulleys were used to guide and support the cable. The cable gripper was automatically attached or detached by a ramp. Wagons ran across points under their own momentum, dropping the cable one side and picking it up again on the other.

19. An unusual steel side tipping wagon used on the 2ft gauge line which carried furnace materials at Goldendale Ironworks, Tunstall, Stoke-on-Trent (5-12-1970). The body looks as though it rolled along the frame to tip, with teeth to keep it in alignment.

20. Bowaters Paper Mills at Sittingbourne had an extensive 2ft 6in gauge system. Among their large fleet of wagons were these all steel either-side tippers, having bodies 108 x 78 x 36in and top hung doors (19-5-1961).

21. J. Parish & Co., at Erith near Gravesend, had a loam (a type of clay) quarry which was connected to a wharf on the Thames by a 4ft gauge line, which used steel end tipping wagons, seen abandoned in the quarry after dumpers had replaced the railway (6-5-1959). Railway equipment was often collected like this and abandoned, sometimes for years, when a quarry closed or (as here) the railway was replaced by dumpers.

Hoppers

An alternative to any kind of tipping wagon is a hopper, with a door either in the wagon floor or along the bottom of a side against a sloping floor.

22. This little 2ft gauge wagon was apparently built on a skip frame by Smith & Sons (Raunds) Ltd as the first railway wagon at Raunds brickworks (25-6-1964). A lever at the end opened the bottom door.

23. A rather more sophisticated 2ft gauge hopper, again apparently built on a skip frame, was at Julius Whitehead, Clayton near Bradford on a short cable hauled line between the clay pit and brickworks (14-3-1970). The body was 70 x 44 max x $35^1/_2$in, with a wheelbase of 21in. The door is certainly well braced. From memory, the wagon was painted pale grey-green. The largely unsupported track on the main incline was laid using grooved rail formerly used on tramways, which was of deep girder section. Unusually, the grooves were placed on the outside of the rails so the flanges of the hopper's wheels did not run in them.

24. Hoveringham Gravel at Hurst Pierrepoint, Nottingham, used steel Hudson side hopper wagons carrying $2^{1}/_{2}$ tons on their 2ft gauge gravel pit railway (28-2-1973). Note the operating lever which opens and closes both door simultaneously.

25. Bowaters at Sittingbourne had steel side hoppers on their 2ft 6in gauge system (19-5-1961). The photograph shows both sides of these wagons, and emphasises the inherent uneven loading on each side. Note that these wagons have hand brakes fitted.

26. The Penmaenmawr & Welsh Granite Co on the North Wales coast used 3ft gauge wooden side hopper wagons, seen in the main line sidings (14-6-1968). Note the lever to operate the door catch at this end (there is a similar lever at the other end), and the way the sloping floor extends below the top of the frames. They held 3 tons 14 cwt and were used to load ships from the pier, or main line wagons. The other side of the wagon had one plank at the base and two planks at the top ie above the sloping floor to support the load, but the middle three planks were not then fitted, although the strapping end plates still had the bolt holes. Note how the nearer rail is laid very close to the face of the retaining wall, to maximise the wagon's overhang over the standard gauge one, and so reduce spillage.

Tipplers and Tubs

Yet another design of bulk mineral wagon dispenses with any kind of door and emptying is by inversion, usually in some sort of rotary tippler. Typically this has a cage to hold the wagon in place on the rails while it is rotated on its longitudinal axis, inverted and emptied, and righted again.

27. The metre gauge railway serving the Loddington Ironstone Co quarries, about 3 miles west of Kettering, used these distinctive tubs until replaced by an extension to the standard gauge line in the late 1950s (11-1-1960). In the foreground are motion parts from an old Sharp Stewart 0-4-0ST which had been recently scrapped.

28. Very similar tubs were used on the 3ft gauge railway serving Eastwell quarries. The illustration shows a tub in the tippler above the main line siding (20-4-1960). The loaded wagon unbalanced the tippler frame which rotated, inverting and so emptying the wagon. Its momentum then brought it right way up again, being stopped by a band brake at the further end of the tippler, operated by the long lever.

29. The Wellingborough Iron Co had modernised their metre gauge railway to the ironstone quarries in the 1930s, with a fleet of steel tippler wagons built by G.R.Turner, of Langley Mill near Nottingham. A sturdy steel four wheeled frame, 13ft 10in x 5ft 7in, with 6ft wheelbase and 2ft diameter wheels, fitted with a lever hand brake and Norwegian couplers, carried a pair of steel boxes 6 x 6 x 4ft, each with a nominal capacity of 5 tons. At the works a specially adapted crane put a pair of slings round the ring at each end of the box, and by lowering one side of the sling assembly was able to rotate and invert the box in the air *(see photo 94)*.

30. Richard Thomas & Baldwins used tippler tubs on the 3ft gauge system serving their ironstone mines at Irthlingborough. The photograph shows original wagons, and those with extended sides to increase the capacity, particularly when loaded by machine. While locomotive haulage was used underground, continuous cable was used in the works yard, with the gripper connection clearly visible (27-5-1965).

31. The smallest gauge I have ever seen was 11in, at the Good Luck lead mine beside the Via Gellia at Cromford near Matlock. A tub is preserved in one of Derby City Museums, in the Silk Mill – Derby's Museum of Industry & History (13-7-1989). The body is two sheets of iron fastened to a floor comprising three planks and a closed end comprising four planks. The other end has a bottom hinged iron door. The underframe was a single thick block of wood to which the axles were bolted. Emptying was by lifting the closed end, probably with the help of a long wooden lever. Note the tall narrow section of the tub, typical of vehicles used where the mineral occurred in narrow vertical veins, so that the wagon was no wider than the man who dug out the ore and pushed the tub. This is in contrast to tubs used to extract minerals occurring in approximately horizontal beds (for example coal and ironstone), where there was little restriction on width although height might be limited, and so tubs could be approximately square section. The diamond shaped 'works plate', dated 1972, seems to have been added by previous owners (probably those who restored it before the tub came to the Museum).

32. (*Opposite Top*) Coalbrookdale is a very old industrial area, and the Ironbridge Gorge Museum Trust operates a number of museums in the area. The Jackfield Tile Museum, Ironbridge, used to have a display showing how clay was mined locally, with several 1ft 10in gauge wooden tubs from one of the Jackfield clay pits (31-7-1998). The body measured 36 x 32 x 14½in, with a length overall of 25½in. The wheels were 9¾in diameter at 16in wheelbase. Note the iron horn on the end to grip the links of the continuous chain used for haulage. Similar horns were fitted to ordinary V-skips used at Whittlesea Central Brick for haulage from the clay pit up to the works.

33. Brookes Ltd, Lightcliffe near Halifax, had a fireclay mine in the bottom of a valley. The 1ft 9in gauge tubs were brought up to the fireclay dump at the works level *(see photo 7)* by means of a ropeway (20-9-1967). The tub fitted in to a special cradle for the journey. At the top of the ropeway (seen here after work had finished for the day, hence the padlocked chain securing the carrier to the framing) the tubs were put back on the rails and pushed along an elevated gantry above the dump, and they were emptied by overturning. The tubs measured $38^{1}/_{2}$ x $26^{1}/_{4}$ x $13^{1}/_{2}$in, with $7^{3}/_{4}$in wheels on a $12^{1}/_{2}$in wheelbase.

34. The 1ft 6$^1/_2$in gauge tubs at Middleton Mining Co had bodies 37 x 28$^1/_2$ x 21, with 9in wheels set at 12$^1/_2$in centres. Note the catch to secure the top hung steel door (1-6-1973).

35. Nearby was the 1ft 5in gauge mine of the Long Rake Spar Co, Youlgrave near Matlock. Its steel tubs had bodies 36 x 24 x 25in high, with 9in wheels on a 16in wheelbase. The floor was about 11in above the rail (1-6-1973).

36. Tubs are still used in small independent mines, as at the Monument Mine in the Forest of Dean (23-8-2001). These 1ft 7$^1/_2$in gauge tubs appear to be made of aluminium, not steel, and had bodies 38 x 31 x 22 (max height 33in), with 9$^1/_2$in wheels at 18in wheelbase. The bar dragging behind is to prevent runaways on the haul up the drift (by the winch on the right). Note the simple  turntable instead of points. The apparatus beside the turntable is a form of tippler, for emptying the tubs down the chute. The wheels of the tub just fit between the flanges of two pieces of steel channel, one either side of the tippler platform, so that when the platform is raised (electrically or hydraulically) the partially inverted tub is supported by the upper flanges of the channel and does not fall *(see photo 109)*.

37. Wedgewood Colliery, Talke near Stoke-on-Trent, was an independent (ie not National Coal Board) 'footrail' or drift mine. The photograph shows a rake of 8 2ft gauge tubs beginning the descent of the 750 yard long main drift, braked by the rope used to haul out the full tubs. The bodies measured 48 x 36 x 21in, with an overall height of 36in, and held 10cwt of coal. The 12in diameter wheels had a wheelbase of 19$^1/_2$in. Note the diamond crossing totally devoid of checkrails in the foreground, followed by a piece of rail which has interesting curvature and gradient!

38. Once locomotive haulage and machine loading became common in coal mines, tubs were found to be very inefficient, due to their small capacity and poor running characteristics. When pits were modernised high capacity mine cars with roller bearings were often introduced. The illustration shows the tippler and empties side of the pit head at Wolstanton Colliery, Newcastle under Lyme (16-6-1973) with 2ft 6in gauge $2^1/_2$ ton mine cars. These were 99 x $47^1/_2$ x 41in, with an overall height of 58in. The 14in diameter wheels had a wheelbase of 42in. Note the coupling. In the foreground is a flat rotating plate 113in diameter, with side guards, to convey the empty mine car to the empties road after it has been pushed out of the tippler by the next full one. Note the L-section girder used to direct the mine cars' wheels on to conventional track on leaving the rotating plate.

39. (Opposite) Several brickworks in and around Bedfordshire used aerial ropeways to carry clay from the pit to the works, often crossing old workings which presented a barrier to a railway line. In the pit the ropeway buckets were automatically lifted from their cradles and put on to flat wagons for locomotive haulage to the working face. They were hauled back and automatically transferred to an empty ropeway carrier to return to the works, where the buckets were inverted and emptied. The illustration shows the interior of the transfer station at Redland Flettons Ltd, Kempston Hardwick, with an empty ropeway bucket about to be lowered on to the short flat 2ft gauge wagon which will carry it to the working face for loading. Note the steel angles across the wagon to locate the bucket, and the full bucket which will run down by gravity as soon as the wagon with the empty bucket is released (13-9-1967).

Opens

Tipplers and tubs are a type of open wagon but usually without doors. However, ordinary open wagons existed too, even for carrying minerals.

40. The 3ft 9in gauge Norden Railway near Corfe Castle used almost square open wagons to carry clay (S. V. F. Leleux, August 1948). The photograph gives a good idea of wooden wagon construction, with heavy timbers morticed together to form the frame, and secured by transverse iron tie rods. The author (aged 9) provides an idea of size!

41. Napton Brickworks near Daventry used 1ft 4in gauge open wagons to carry clay (30-5-1966). The photograph was taken after the railway had been dumped in an old part of the quarry, having been replaced by an earth mover. A side door wagon is in the foreground, with its door leaning against the truck behind, while DOBBIN is an end door wagon. Most of the wagons here were named! Originally the railway ran all the way from clay pit to works, and then wagons had a horn on the closed end to grip the haulage chain. End door wagons had bodies 42 x 27$\frac{1}{2}$ /25$\frac{1}{2}$ wide x 16$\frac{1}{2}$ in, and the side door wagons were very similar: 42 x 28/26 x 17$\frac{1}{2}$ in. Both had 7$\frac{1}{2}$ in diameter wheels and a wheelbase of 20$\frac{1}{2}$ in.

42. During the First World War the War Department bought large numbers of 60cm gauge open wagons for use in supplying the front line. Some later found their way into the hands of all kinds of industrial users, from Joseph Arnold's sand quarries (for bags of dried sand) to the farms supplying potatoes for Smith's Crisps. Some went to British military establishments. This wooden framed and bodied bogie wagon at Ministry of Defence Lydd Ranges near Dungeness was the 1939 version. Note the sprung bogies and the hand brake at one end (14-8-1978).

43. The Air Force bomb dump at Fauld near Burton-on-Trent was served by an extensive 2ft gauge system. Amongst its large fleet of wagons were a number of all steel bogie opens by Robert Hudson. Both sides and the end away from the brake pillar could be removed to make a flat wagon (3-7-1973).

44. George Garside at Leighton Buzzard had a steel open wagon. Originally the body was wooden, but after some years a new steel body was made, presumably to the same dimentions. Built on a skip frame, the body ends were fixed and supported by a pair of vertical angle irons welded to the frame, and the doors either side lifted out, being secured by a pair of pegs fitting into holes in horizontal steel bars across the wooden floor (4-1-1961). It was used by the engineers to carry tools and materials around the extensive quarry workings.

45. Ministry of Defence railways often had large numbers of Hudson slat sided open 'ammunition' wagons. At Fauld after closure there was a line of 61 of them beside the depot road. This wagon, on the late Ted Boston's railway at Cadeby near Nuneaton, was probably one of the first to be preserved (19-6-1965). Note the slat sides, the strengthening angles and the lever operated hand brake.

46. The Welsh slate quarries used simple robust iron open wagons to remove the vast quantities of waste slate (rubbish) from the quarries and the slate mills. These wagons at Maenoffferen Quarry, Blaenau Festiniog are typical (19-8-1963). Their bodies were 72$\frac{1}{2}$in x 37 x 18in or 72$\frac{1}{2}$in x 42$\frac{1}{2}$in x 30$\frac{1}{4}$in, both with a wheelbase of 22$\frac{1}{2}$in, with the axle 21in from the closed end. The smaller wagons  were far more common; I suspect that these deeper wagons were an attempt to increase carrying capacity but were then too heavy for men to move or tip easily. I never saw large wagons like these in any other slate quarry. Rubbish wagons were emptied by up-ending at the end of the tip. Wagons used in quarries which had workings in deep pits as well as, or instead of, along galleries (levels) had a lifting eye at each corner of the body, so that the wagons could be hoisted into the workings by the overhead cableways ('Blondins'). Also visible in the picture are some of the flat trolleys used to carry large blocks of slate from the quarry to the mill. Note the double flanged wheels used extensively in the Welsh slate quarries.

47. The metre gauge Wellingborough Iron Co had an ash wagon, apparently home made on a standard ore tippler chassis (5-5-1965). The body was 13ft 7in x 8ft 1in/5ft 11in x 2ft 1in. The holes in the end suggest that it could be removable. On another occasion a standard chassis carried a body one plank high containing sleepers for the permanent way gang.

48. Peat wagons also often had slat sides. On smaller systems such as Country Kitchen Foods at Wilmslow, Cheshire, the 2ft gauge wagons were small, wooden and not well maintained (13-7-1974). In the foreground is a home made prefabricated length of curved track, to connect the sidings between the rows of drying peat blocks with the main line. The three sleepers (spacers would seem a better term), appear to be pieces of steel angle welded on.

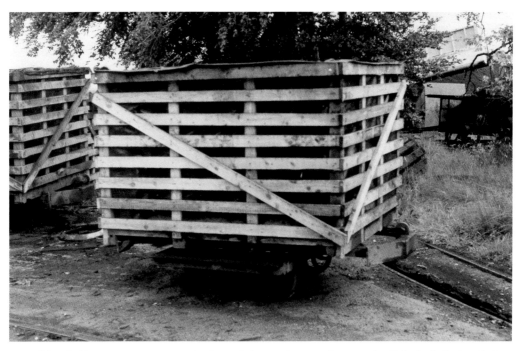

49. This 2ft 6in gauge wagon at L&P Peat, Solway Moss works near Carlisle had obviously just received heavy repair if not reconstruction (16-8-1994). The body, of 3 x 1in timber, was 72 x 62 x 48in. The frame extended 11in at each end and the wheelbase was 23in.

50. Not far away, Boothby Peat had steel 2ft gauge wagons, with both lattice and solid sides (16-8-1994). The lattice bodies were 86 x 60^1/$_2$ x 54in, and the solid ones 97 x 64 x 54in.

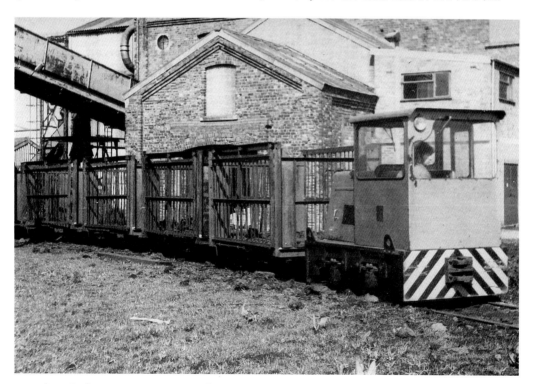

51. Fisons' 3ft gauge system at Hatfield near Doncaster used slat sided steel wagons, with top hung side doors which swung outwards when the wagon was tilted in the tippler (2-4-1977). Here they are being shunted by a 43hp Hunslet diesel (7367) delivered in 1974.

Flats

52. Collieries made extensive use of flat wagons to carry materials underground. Here in the stockyard at Chatterley Whitfield Colliery, Stoke-on-Trent, a 2ft gauge 30DLG Ruston (385900) shunts a flat wagon loaded with steel girders for supporting underground roadways, and an open wagon apparently made from a mine car (26-4-1971). Note the couplings, particularly the long bar so that the girders on the flat wagon will not foul the locomotive.

53. The smallest wheels I have ever seen were on this 2ft gauge pipe carrier, used on a tunnelling contract by NJK Construction Co.Ltd at Lawkholme Lane, Keighley (23-7-1969). The trolley was 47 x 23in, with $3^1/_2$in diameter wheels on 34in wheelbase. The pairs of bolsters were $2^1/_2$in wide and $7^1/_2$in apart. The flat was 64 x 21in, with 12in wheels and 34in wheelbase. The actual floor was 47 x 23in. The detachable bodies were 4 x 3 x 2ft (note the lifting eyes) and 4 x 2 x 2ft, with lifting holes at the upper corners.

54. Norcon Ltd, at Ripley near Guildford, used skip frames boarded over to carry concrete pipes on the 2ft gauge railway within their plant (7-9-1967). The locomotive is Orenstein & Koppel 6193.

55. The Admiralty's Chattenden & Upnor Railway, near Chatham, was 2ft 6in gauge. It had several flat wagons, one here seen loaded with ballast after being sold to the Welshpool & Llanfair Railway(10-10-1975). Note the brakes on each bogie. The body measured 23ft 10^1/$_2$in x 6ft 8^1/$_2$in, with ends 2ft/2ft 9in tall and side height 6in.

56. *(Above)* The commonest wagons on Bowaters' 2ft 6in gauge railway at Sittingbourne were steel framed bogie flat wagons with wooden floors and ends (19-5-1961). They were used for carrying bales of wood pulp and rolls of finished paper. Many were built by the Butterley Company, at Ripley near Derby.

57. *(Left)* The 2ft 6in gauge steel bogie wagons built by Gloucester Carriage & Wagon for British Steel at Shotton had to be sturdy, as the steel coils weighed 10 to 14 tons each. (14-4-1972). The wagons were 25ft x 5ft 9in, with frames of 12 x 4in channel. The bogies had 2ft 3in diameter wheels and 4ft wheelbase, and were placed at approximately 18ft centres.

58. European Systems, Derby, operated a 3ft gauge line to move materials within their engineering works. The photograph shows the entire locomotive and rolling stock - two of each - days before the whole lot was auctioned following closure (1-7-2002). The bogies were 18ft 5in x 6ft 0in with the floor 2ft $5^{1}/_{2}$in above the rail. The steel coupling bar was $3^{1}/_{2}$in diameter with the coupling holes at 9ft 8in centres.

59. Sir Lindsey Parkinson briefly operated an industrial building plant on the Wellingborough Ironworks site, with a 3ft gauge railway to carry building panels around the works (1-9-1965).

60. British Insulated Callendars Cables, at Belvedere near Gravesend had a 3ft 6$\frac{1}{2}$in gauge system within the factory and up to the wharf. As the usual traffic was drums of cable, there was a fleet of concave flat wagons (if that is not a contradiction) so that the drums would rest securely without need for additional fastening (27-2-1960). The wagons were coupled using long steel bars (just visible between the first two wagons).

Tanks

61. Machines need fuel, and this may be difficult to carry into a quarry. George Garside at Leighton Buzzard adapted several 2ft gauge skip frames to carry a 40 gallon oil drum and simple hand pump to take fuel to their excavators (4-1-1961). The light rail is supported on cut down main line sleepers.

62. At another quarry George Garside simply mounted a rectangular tank on a skip frame (26-10-1965). Note the simple buffer stop, a length of stout timber partly buried in the sand, with a girder clamped across the rails to brace it. Note, too, the scotch under the wagon wheels.

63. Country Kitchen Foods at Wilmslow used two spare underframes, one from a skip and one from a wooden peat wagon, as supports for oil tanks in the works yard (26-2-1974). Narrow gauge wagons are not always found on the rails in industrial premises!

64. Fisons' Peat works at Swinefleet near Doncaster used rectangular tank wagons on its 3ft gauge line to take fuel out to machines on the bog (2-4-1977).

Air Compressors

65. *(Top)* The difficulty of bringing fuel into a quarry has already been mentioned. There is a similar problem if the excavator hits harder material in an otherwise soft bed of sand or clay. Blasting may then be necessary, which requires shot holes to be drilled. At Leighton Buzzard, Joseph Arnold first surmounted this problem by fitting wide steel channel either side of a skip frame so that a standard trailer air compressor could be mounted on it (8-1-1960). Later the firm rebuilt a 20 hp Motor Rail locomotive as a mobile air compressor.

66. *(Middle)* Raunds Brickworks near Wellingborough also had a compressor built on a 2ft gauge skip frame. This seems to have been used more to power pneumatic spades rather than rock drills (23-6-1965).

67. *(Bottom)* Perhaps the most remarkable air compressor was at Wheatley's Trent Vale Tile Works, Newcastle-under-Lyme (30-5-1972). This was a standard commercial compressor with road wheels removed and mounted on a new underframe, carried on six wheels – a short wheelbase bogie at one end and a single pair of wheels at the other. This was presumably to enable it to negotiate sharp curves easily. Note, too, the short piece of chain under the wheel to prevent it running away, a very common practice.

Transporters

Sometimes it saves handling, and therefore time, damage and money, if one vehicle can be carried complete by another. The carrying transporter wagon has to be designed for ease of loading and unloading.

68. The London Brick Co at Arlesey Works near Hitchin had a 2ft 11in gauge line forming a continuous circuit between the kilns and stacking ground. Small overhead electric locomotives, built by LBC themselves, hauled trains of two bogie well wagons (21-4-1958). Each well wagon carried two flat wagons based on skip frames (probably 2ft gauge). These were loaded at, or even in, the kiln and then pushed on to the transporter wagons for the journey to the stacking ground. Here were more temporary tracks, terminating in a short ramp to bring the rails level with the transporter's floor. The transporters were 13ft 8in long over the main frames. While I did not see this anywhere else, the IRS Pocket Books suggest that it was used at several LBC works.

69. In Fletton, on the southern outskirts of Peterborough, the London Brick Co operated a number of brickworks. Many were self contained, but Hicks No 2 works obtained its 'green' (unfired) bricks from a nearby works. At the brick making plant the bricks were loaded on to trolleys, which were themselves then loaded on to 2ft 11in gauge transporter wagons with very low floors for transport to the kiln (23-3-1960). At the kiln the trolleys were wheeled off the wagon on to a low platform and straight into the kiln where there were stacked for firing. The empty trolleys were then taken back by train to the brick making plant. The transporters were roofed so that the bricks would not be damaged in wet weather. The trains were hauled by a cut down Sentinel geared steam locomotive (7701), just visible between the two rakes of wagons.

Special Wagons

70. In North Wales, cut slates were mainly carried in wagons having openwork sides, possibly of iron, possibly of wood horizontals spaced by cast iron bobbins. The Dinorwic version with wooden horizontals is illustrated (26-8-1963). The double flanged wheels used in most of the slate quarries in North Wales might have been tolerant of track gauge but caused complications at points. On hand operated sections of the 1ft $10^3/_4$in gauge Dinorwic system points used special cast iron plates with raised edges to guide the outside of the wheel flanges as the wheel ran on its flanges over the plates. The switches were simple pivoted bars, kicked into position. At the crossing itself the wheels again rested on their flanges. Note the ordinary track here, just steel bars laid on their edge resting in slots cut in the wooden sleepers. On locomotive worked sections there were stub points, with the switch rails and the pivoted rail at the crossing operated through rodding by the same lever.

71. Bradford Waterworks at Chellow Heights on the Haworth Road used an electric 2ft gauge crane to lift dirty sand from the filter beds (3-7-1970).

72. Elkington Copper at Walsall refined copper electrically. The metal was made into blocks with 'wings' for use as anodes in the refining process. These anodes were carried round the site on 2ft 6in gauge wagons fitted with a pair of parallel bars on which the wings rested (20-7-1966). While most of the anode wagons had 4 wheels there was, on that occasion, an experimental bogie version as well.

73. The need for London Underground to keep its tunnels clean is well known. The 2ft gauge Post Office tube had the same need, and it too constructed a vacuum clearer wagon for the purpose (27-2-1973).

74. The 2ft gauge snowplough at Fauld ammunition dump looks home made (3-7-1973). The front tank was probably for water to give additional weight. The rear tank has a removable lid so might have contained salt, particularly in view of the central handrail. Note the front coupling hook, and the provision of a crane hook attachment bar so that it could be lifted and turned round easily, necessary as there was a double track main line.

75. Readymix lorries are common on construction sites, but they cannot go underground. When Mowlem had the contract to construct the tunnel for a water pipeline at Ambergate near Derby they used this 60cm gauge Muhlhauser concrete wagon to take supplies into the tunnel (9-6-1983). A Clayton $5^1/_2$ ton battery electric locomotive (73026) hauled it.

76. Many brickworks dried the green bricks in hot air ovens before firing them. The bricks were placed on flat sheets of metal, themselves laid in the racks on the wagon (much like the trolleys for trays of dirty crockery in some cafeteria). The loaded wagon was pushed into the oven and eventually emerged from the far end, where several brick cars would be made into a train to go to the kiln. The noisy rattle of a train of empty cars was indescribable! The illustration shows a 2ft gauge train of six empty brick cars at Crowborough brickworks, Sussex, hauled by a Lister diesel locomotive (10249) (19-8-1968).

77. L&P Peat, Solway Moss works near Carlisle, made themselves a portable gas welding kit which could be easily transported over their 2ft 6in gauge railway to equipment out on the bog (16-8-1994). The locomotive is Motor Rail 21619 with L&P-built body.

78. Some goods have to be kept dry. Roofed brick transporters have already been illustrated. Another type of user was the Ministry of Defence in ammunition dumps and similar sites, where vans were often provided. These two came from the 2ft 6in gauge railway at Royal Naval Armament Depot at Trecwn, near Fishguard, but were subsequently regauged to 2ft for use on the Golden Valley Railway, which shares part of the standard gauge Midland Railway Centre's site at Butterley near Derby. The Baguley Drewry battery electric locomotive (3703) came from another ammunition dump system (18-5-1997).

79. This 3ft gauge bogie wagon, with steel frame and wooden bogies, was built in the 1930s to carry the jib of an excavator into the ironstone quarry at Hanging Houghton, six miles north of Northampton and close to Scaldwell quarries (24-7-1962). During World War II the railway was replaced by a standard gauge line and everything was just abandoned. This siding ran between two hedges. When I first found this line, a couple of years before, the two hedges had grown together and the wagons were inside a long thicket. Photographs were impossible except in winter, when the leaves had fallen. At least the further hedge had been trimmed by this visit! Among the derelict side tippers beyond was at least one carrying a plate McLachlan & Co, Darlington.

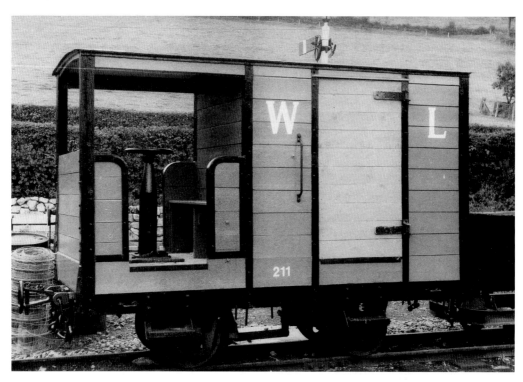

80. The Welshpool & Llanfair Railway obtained a lot of rolling stock from the Chattenden & Upnor Railway, near Chatham, when it closed, not least because there were not many sources of 2ft 6in gauge equipment left in the UK. Among its acquisitions was this little brake van, which appears to have included accommodation for small items of goods as well (10-10-1975).

Coaches

Surprising as it may seem, quite a few industrial railways had passenger vehicles. Some were built to take important visitors around the site and others were genuine works transport. The large Dinorwic and Penrhyn slate quarries in North Wales each ran a regular train morning and evening for their quarrymen for years until about 1950, when the men no longer needed it.

81. The Guinness Brewery in Dublin had an extensive 1ft 10in gauge system, with a fleet of unusual steam locomotives having the cylinders on top of the boiler. The photograph shows one (No 15), preserved in the works yard, together with a 4-wheel knife board coach (7-9-1960). Note the frame for an awning. In view of the relatively compact nature of the site, I suspect this coach was for important visitors.

82. At Solway Moss near Carlisle, L&P Peat had a small vehicle, stored off the 2ft 6in gauge rails, with a single longitudinal seat and curved corrugated iron roof. With a horizontal handrail at each end it looks as though it could be pushed as well as hauled by a locomotive (16-8-1994). British Moss at Hatfield works near Doncaster had a similar 3ft gauge coach with central back to back seating, built for a special visit but, sadly, it was very prone to derailment so was not greatly used.

83. The 2ft 6in gauge Chattenden & Upnor Railway has been featured several times already. It, too, ran passenger trains. In 1941 Cravens built some pretty basic 5-compartment bogie coaches, here seen on the Welshpool & Llanfair (2-9-1961). I rode in one of these coaches from Llanfair back to Welshpool in a strong cold wind on the Preservation Society's AGM Special in March 1962, and the open construction ensured passengers became frozen through! A coach with similar roof and ends but longitudinal seating became a station shelter on the C&UR.

84. The Admiralty operated C&UR also owned a magnificent modern coach with brake compartment for the guard, complete with the line's crest on the body panel, but then the Navy does have a reputation for appearances (9-3-1960)!

85. Bowaters ran a scheduled passenger service over their 2ft 6in gauge railway linking the different parts of their works at Sittingbourne (19-5-1961). The coaches were converted from the bogie flat wagons, and had longitudinal seats along each side.

86. Coach 394 at Lydd Ranges was more in the nature of a mobile office, with desks fastened to the walls (14-8-1978). Its body measured 13ft x 4ft 5$^{1}/_{2}$in x 5ft 5in/6ft 2in high. The eaves were 7ft 4in above the rail.

87. At Fauld, the Ministry of Defence had several Hudson coaches for internal transport over the 2ft gauge railway (3-7-1973).

88. Wedgewood Colliery, Talke near Stoke-on-Trent was a private drift mine ('footrail') served by a 2ft gauge railway. Miners were taken along the main drift on this rake of manriders built by Sheepbridge (7-10-1975). The bodies were 11ft 6in x 3ft 9in, top of side 25in above the rail and 3ft 9in wheelbase. Note the pulley between the rails to support the haulage cable and the irregular rail alignment between the two points.

89. Richard Thomas & Baldwins converted a pair of 3ft gauge ore tubs to manriders at their Irthlingborough mines (22-11-1965). The two tubs were permanently coupled by a pivoted steel bar and a pair of crossed chains.

Track – General

Some industrial narrow gauge railways had track which would have done credit to a public passenger carrying line, but on many systems the trackwork was merely sufficient for their purposes. While derailments are annoying and time wasting, track materials are not cheap and neither is labour for track maintenance. Most narrow gauge industrial railways used light flat bottom rail, typically 20 to 60lb per yard (main line rails typically weigh 95 to 110lb per yard). Sleepers were generally wood or pressed steel. Ballast was definitely optional! While Kempston Hardwick Brickworks used crushed brick ballast many lines just laid track on the ground, and weeds or dirt held everything in position.

90. Great Row Colliery, Peacock Hay near Kidsgrove, was an independent 'footrail' served by a 1ft 10in gauge railway. The winding house on the left of the photograph hauled rakes of 4 full tubs from the drift (off to the right) into the left hand loop (2-10-1975). When two full rakes were in the loop the haulage cable was taken round some pulleys behind the photographer so that the full tubs could be hauled up the short steep gradient to the tippler. The empties were then lowered into the right hand loop for return to the mine. Note the gradient, the worn rail losing its head by the point, the lack of a point lever – indeed, looking at it, I doubt whether the blades needed to be moved very often, as the full tubs could trail through the switches and the empties would tend to take the straight route. Spare wagons lie beside the line, and nearby is the supply of pit props.

91. A lot of 2ft and narrower gauge track used in mines, quarries and construction sites was supplied in prefabricated lengths, straights, curves (several radii) and points, just like the track for a toy train set, and for precisely the same reason. Such track could be laid, modified, moved and taken up for reuse elsewhere with very little effort. The illustration

shows 1ft 6in gauge track at an access shaft for a sewer contract undertaken by C. V. Buchan in Stoke-on-Trent (22-7-1972). The points were 12ft radius, with the inner rails of the loop only 9in apart (hence one reason why mining equipment is usually narrow and the frames carrying the wheel bearings are inside the wheels, to save space. The inverted braced steel sheets behind are 12ft x 4ft, and have the rails for a passing loop welded on the other face.

92. Check rails were sometimes laid outside the running rails, to encourage wagons to keep on the rails, as here at Lowland Colliery, Kidsgrove, Staffordshire (19-4-1971). The gradient was about 1 in 2, and the sideways pull of the haulage rope might have pulled the leading tubs off the rails of the branch. Note the block of wood in the straight flangeway to keep the point open, and the hinged steel 'Warwick' bar which normally guards the entrance to the adit from runaways. 2ft gauge.

93. *(Opposite)* Occasionally standard gauge track materials would be used. On the Wellingborough Iron Co metre gauge line, a sharp curve approaching the tunnel under the Midland main line was check railed and laid in bullhead rail, probably because the special chairs required for the check rail were common on standard gauge installations and were easily obtainable (1-9-1965).

94. Catch points were sometimes provided, where there were particularly steep gradients near hazardous situations, for example level crossings or, as here at Wellingborough, a long sharp curve *(see 93)*. The points were normally sprung to deflect any runaway off the track. Ascending trains just pushed through them, and a workman had to operate a lever to close the points when a descending train passed. Note the unusual use of concrete sleepers on this section of metre gauge track (1-9-1965). In the background is the crane with special slings used to empty the 'boxes' of iron ore *(see photo 29)*. One is being inverted.

95. Industrial sidings usually just finished, or petered out in the dirt, but occasionally neat buffer stops were provided, like this one at York Sewage Works (1-3-1969). The buffer beam was 9 x 6 x 36in, 9in above the rails.

Points

96. The points at passing loops points might have weighted levers, so that trains could push the blades open in the trailing direction but the lever would hold the points set for trains in the facing direction. Alternatively a spring might be fitted instead of a lever, as at Storton's gravel pit, Northampton (17-8-1968). The standard of track, more or less straight and level, was typical of 2ft gravel pits lines.

97. The standard 2ft gauge prefabricated point was either left hand or right hand, but Berrylands Sewage Works near Kingston had a 3-way point (24-8-1969). Note that there are no operating levers. This was common – a well aimed kick was quite as effective! The pressed steel sleepers are clearly visible. The Scaldwell ironstone quarry system also had a 3-way point in its depot, complete with two levers and a plank walkway over the rodding.

98. At the other end of the scale were conventional points in heavy rail just like ones on the main line. This 3ft gauge example was laid in the factory floor at European Systems, Derby. Note the operating lever which is also flush with the floor until it is raised for use, and the steel angle forming the inner edge of the flangeways, with steel bracing strips between the moving switch rails (1-7-2002).

99. Sometimes, and on some systems not infrequently, it was necessary to gain access to a temporary siding from the main line. Installing a conventional point would mean disturbing the main track and involve a lot of labour. Accordingly, various types of portable point were developed, which could just drop on top of the main track to connect with the new siding. Fisons' Swinefleet Works near Doncaster made this short ramp with tapered rails (2-4-1977). The two spacers had lugs which fitted inside the heads of the main rails, keeping it in position. Ordinary curved track, supported on blocks of wood, was then bolted on to the ramp and gave access to the siding. Such a point could be used by a light locomotive such as a Lister diesel. Unfortunately the main track, although undisturbed, was blocked, so the point would have to be removed to permit passage.

100. An alternative was a double ended ramp which included a conventional point in the raised section. Laid over the rails, trains could cross it on the main line or be diverted to the branch. The 1ft 8in gauge example illustrated is an exhibit at the Irchester Narrow Gauge Museum near Wellingborough (27-8-2001). It was formerly used on the portable railway employed to service the filter beds at Ravensthorpe Reservoir, 7 miles north west of Northampton.

Turntables

101. The alternative to points, particularly on hand operated lines, was to use turntables. The most basic design was simply a flat pivoted plate, with short guard rails at the edge of the plate linking each pair of exit tracks, as here at Berrylands Sewage Works where the plate was 42in diameter (27-10-1975). A wagon would be pushed on to the table, stopped and pushed round to the new track.

102. An alternative was to use a turning plate dropped over main tracks. This comprised a steel base which supported the pivoted table. The table had one side extended to make a short ramp with flanges which fitted outside the main track's railheads to maintain alignment. A skip was pushed up the ramp until it balanced on the table and the flanges of the ramp were lifted clear of the rails. The table was then turned and the wagon pushed down the ramp on to the other track. Such a table, 2ft gauge, and a rail-less turntable, are seen in the filter beds at Bradford Waterworks on Thornton Moor (20-7-1970). Wagons were hauled up the ramp, or lowered down it, by a wire rope run round a pulley at the top and attached to the locomotive.

103. Wagon turntables could have just a single pair of tracks crossing or two pairs at right angles, so that there was always track across the table in both directions. An example of the latter on 2ft gauge is seen at Bradford Waterworks, Thornton Moor (20-7-1970). Note the spider with rollers which supports the actual table and makes it easy to turn. The unit had probably been partially dismantled to make it easier to remove and install. The railway had a number of shallow circular wells beside the filter beds to locate the turntables when required, and bridged by short lengths of track when not is use. One such bridged well is just in front of the locomotive and another is just behind it.

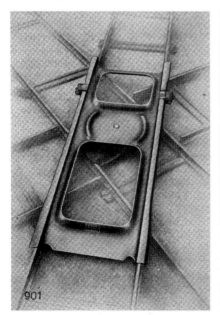

The London based light railway engineers M. E. Engineering Ltd. imported these "Meco" portable turntables from Germany in quantity during the 1950's for use on temporary lines on contract sites, clay pits, peat bogs etc. *(Andrew Neale Collection)*

Crossings

104. Many industrial premises had both standard gauge and narrow on site, and inevitably sometimes they had to cross. At Chatterley Whitfield Colliery, Stoke-on-Trent, the 2ft gauge line in the stock yard crossed several standard gauge tracks en route to the pit head (3-8-1972). Note that the 2ft gauge rails are slightly higher than the standard gauge ones, and in most places there was no flangeway provided for the narrow gauge wheels – they simply rode across the standard gauge rails on their flanges, so the train bounced across! Two men walked beside the train to make sure it kept on the rails while crossing.

105. Sometimes when two gauges crossed the crossing was made entirely in standard gauge bullhead rail, as at Knostrop Sewage Works, Leeds, where the 2ft gauge crossed a standard gauge line to the nearby power station and a colliery. The lighter narrow gauge rail on the approach track can just be seen in the foreground, and beyond the crossing (27-3-1970).

106. If the narrow gauge was rather higher than the standard then a pivoted length of track, rather like a gate, could be used, as on this 2ft gauge hand operated line at Dorking Lime, Betchworth (2-3-1960). Note the walkway between the rails.

Emptying Methods

107. Some tipplers have been illustrated already with the wagons. These are some simpler examples. One method is to put a stout length of timber longitudinally under a wagon and use it as a lever to upend the wagon, particularly a tub, as at Monument Colliery, Forest of Dean (23-8-2001), or the little wagons at Napton Brickworks *(see photo 41).*

108. Alternatively, at the tip the ends of the rails are curved into the shape of a cup-hook. When the tub is pushed along the leading wheels drop into the loop, halting the wagon and slightly dropping one end. The other end is then lifted to empty it, as seen at Wedgwood Colliery, Talke near Stoke-on-Trent (7-10-1975). 2ft gauge.

109. Tipplers which lift and partially invert the tub have already been mentioned. The illustration shows one emptying a 2ft gauge tub at Great Row Colliery, Kidsgrove, Staffordshire (8-10-1975).

Derailments

110. Unfortunately derailments can occur on any railway. At least narrow gauge wagons are usually small and relatively light, so they can often be lifted or levered back on to the rails. This derailment of 2ft gauge skips of sand in Joseph Arnold's yard, Leighton Buzzard needed the skips to be shovelled empty before they could be righted and rerailed (10-4-1961). If a derailed skip remained upright and more or less in line with the track then rerailing ramps were used. These were V-shaped castings with side pieces. The apex had a pair of lugs to fit over the rail head, and the two ramps would be put as close as possible to the leading derailed wheels. When the locomotive pulled the wagon towards the apex of the ramp the wheels were guided by the side pieces and ran up the ramp, to fall back on to the rails. Quarry locomotives often carried these ramps for immediate use.

(Opposite Top) Bowaters had a 2ft 6in gauge system linking their paper mills at Sittingbourne and Kemsey with the company's harbour at Ridham Dock, a total distance of about 3 miles. It operated a scheduled service of passenger trains for employees. Here, one of the large 0-6-2T used on the main line, ALPHA (Bagnall 2472 of 1932) waits at the dock with a mixed train for Sittingbourne comprising 3 bogie flat wagons and 4 coaches (themselves converted from flat wagons, with longitudinal seats against the sides) (11-6-1960).

(Opposite Bottom) George Garside had a quarry at Grovebury, on the outskirts of Leighton Buzzard, which supplied sand direct to a neighbouring roofing tile works. A 20hp Motor Rail diesel locomotive pushes a train of 2ft gauge 1yd^3 skips back to the sand pit from the tile works (29-6-1961).

An example of economical track repair on the main line of the 2ft gauge Leighton Buzzard Light Railway is shown (14-5-1988). At the time it was photographed, this length of the former main line near Stonehenge Works was used as a siding by the Preservation Society, but I had noted this joint (and others like it!) in 1960 while doing research for my history of the LBLR, at a time when the sand trains were still running frequently. It looks as though the replacement rail was just too short, so a convenient off-cut was used to bridge the gap, the whole being held secure by the fishplates and spikes, although there seems to have been a local shortage of fishplate bolts too! Note how the rail head has worn, to the extent that wheel flanges have worn away a lot of the left hand fishplate.

TIPPING TRUCKS

Illustration No. 1606

Illustration No. 1613

HUDSON
LIGHT RAILWAY
EQUIPMENT

MINING TRUCKS

•

ESTATE TRUCKS

Illustration No. 1607

Illustration No. 1614

WE ALSO PRODUCE

STEEL CASTINGS
IN OUR OWN FOUNDRY

Robert Hudson Ltd was the largest manufacturer of light railway plant in the world and this bold advertisement in "The Engineer" of 17 August 1945 shows examples of the three most common types of wagon – side tipping "V skips" in two foot and standard gauge, sugar cane cars and pit tubs. *(Andrew Neale Collection)*